STUDENT GUIDE FOR ETHNICITY AND PSYCHOLOGY

African-, Asian-, Latino- and Native-American Psychologies
Revised Printing

Kenneth P. Monteiro
San Francisco State University

with

Mary Garrette
Perry Ancheta
Raquel Lisette Baker
James Daniel
Sherry Loewinger
Galin Luk
Jonathan Rosenberg
Edmond Seban
Stephanie Smith
Frank Starks
Joanne M. Spinardi
Nathan G. Yrizarry

KENDALL/HUNT PUBLISHING COMPANY
4050 Westmark Drive   Dubuque, Iowa 52002

Contents

Native American Psychology

African-American Psychology

❖   ❖   ❖

Black Psychology
Maulana Karenga

Multiple Choice

(pp. 21)

1. Which of the following events occurred in conjunction with the first Black Ph.D. in Psychology?
   a. Blacks began to publish research to disprove racists charges of Black inferiority
   b. Blacks pushed for stronger departments of psychology in Black schools
   c. Blacks attempted to provide better psychological services to the Black community
   d. all the above

(pp. 22)

2. The Association of Black Psychologist (ABP) was founded in 1968 in _____ the American Psychological Association
   a. protest of
   b. conjunction with
   c. in spite of
   d. none of the above.

(pp. 23)

3. The first Non-White President of the American Psychology Association was.
   a. Price Cobbs
   b. Wade Nobles
   c. Kenneth Clark
   d. Stanley G. Hall

(pp. 22)

4. Which of the following is **NOT** a school in Black Psychology?
   a. traditional
   b. transitional
   c. racial
   d. reformist

1

(pp. 23)

5. Several Black social scientist including Amos Wilson and Wade Nobles argue that in order to understand the psychology of Black people the behavior scientist must begin the study in:
   a. Africa
   b. the rural south
   c. slavery
   d. the genes

(pp. 24)

6. When Grier and Cobbs speak about the "shadows of the past" they are referring to _____
   a. Black power
   b. slavery
   c. socio-economic power
   d. KKK

(pp. 31)

7. The key concepts in Linda James Myers contribution to an Afrocentric psychology are _____ and _____
   a. community and communalistic
   ᴄ. optimality and suboptimality
   c. collective and individualistic
   d. economics and political

(pp. 23)

8. Which is **NOT** a defining aspects of the reformist school of Black psychology ?
   a. maintain all the concerns for white attitudes.
   b. focuses more on attitudinal change rather than changes in public policy
   c. combines an Afrocentric psychology with an Eurocentric psychology.
   d. all of the above.

(pp. 26)

9. The idea of "confused knowledge about a people with knowledge of a people" is a _____ view.
   a. reformist
   b. traditional
   c. victims
   d. radical

(pp. 33)   10. One of the most controversial and discussed theories in the area of Black psychology is _____
    a. The Cress Theory of Color-Confrontation and Racism
    b. Black Rage
    c. Why Blacks Kill Blacks
    d. Toward a Black Psychology

Short Answers

(pp. 21)   1. Why does the author purposely omit the study of animal behavior as part of the definition of psychology?

(pp. 22-23)   2. Briefly discuss the concerns of Black Psychology

(pp. 21)   3. Why was Francis Sumner important to Black Psychology?

(pp. 24-25)   4. According to Alvin Poussaint, what is the reason for Black violence against Blacks?

(pp. 22-23)   5. Briefly compare and contrast the three schools of Black Psychology.

(pp. 25)   6. According to Charles Thomas, what is "instructive intervention"?

(pp. 29-30)   7. What are definitional systems? Why are they important to Black Psychology? Discuss briefly.

(pp. 36)   8. Explain the metaphor of "matadors" in relationship to Black Psychology

(pp. 22)   9. Discuss briefly the Association of Black Psychologist (ABP) and its purpose.

(pp. 34)   10. Discuss briefly the relationship between melanin and the development of the Black child.

Black Self-Hatred Paradigm Revisited:
An Africentric Analysis

Joseph A. Baldwin, Raeford Brown and Reginald Hopkins

Multiple Choice

(pp. 45)   1. Which statement is **FALSE?** The "Black Self-Hatred Paradigm"
describes . . .
  a. the construct of black self hatred.
  b. a conceptual framework which uses Eurocentric
methodologies and assumptions.
  c. the nature of "black self concept" in relation to African culture.
  d. the existence of cultural homogeneity between Africans and
Europeans.

(pp. 41-42)   2. According to the article, the "Black Self-Hatred" thesis was **NOT**
able to meet which of the following of its intended purposes?
  a. to accurately describe the development of black self concept.
  b. to accurately predict black behavior.
  c. to create intervention strategies for "black self-hatred" .
  d. all of the above

(pp. 41-42)   3. Which of the following points was NOT made in the article:
  a. Culture plays a significant role in describing and interpreting self-
concept.
  b. Eurocentric models meaningfully explain African-American
experience
  c. The Black Self-Hatred Paradigm misrepresents "black self
conception" in African-Americans
  d. all of the above

(pp. 43-44)   4. According to the article, which of the following is an assumption of
the Eurocentric model?
  a. control and mastery over nature
  b. survival of the fittest
  c. competition
  d. all of the above

(pp. 43-44)   5. The Eurocentric "self" is NOT based on the criterion of a _____ orientation to reality.
    a. external
    b. spiritual
    c. materialistic
    d. physical

(pp. 41-42)   6. Which are examples of how African cultural values shape African-American behavior?
    a. the call response pattern in black churches
    b. African-Americans seek out individualized rather than group experiences
    c. the reverence for the elderly in the African-American community
    d. both a and c

(pp. 45)   7. Which form of empirical evidence is the most widely cited in support of the "Black Self-Hatred" thesis?
    a. Clinical case studies
    b. Field Observations
    c. Racial Preference Studies
    d. Anecdotal Evidence

(pp. 49)   8. Which of the following were cited as evidence for the "Black Self-Hatred" thesis in the clinical field observations and anecdotal evidence?
    a. conflict over skin color in African-American communities
    b. conflict over physical features among African-Americans
    c. the presence in African-Americans of anger and hostility towards whites
    d. all of the above

(pp. 45-48)   9. Which of the following was NOT a finding of the first, Pre-1965, Racial Preference Studies used to support the "Black Self-Hatred" thesis?
    a. Black children tend to draw pictures of Blacks in a positive manner.
    b. Black children tend to choose white dolls as self representation.
    c. Black children tend to value white dolls over brown dolls.
    d. Some Black children choose white or lighter colors over darker ones as self-representation.

(pp. 47-48)   10.   Which of the following conclusions were found in both the Pre-1965 and Post-1965 Racial Preference Studies?
   a.   Black children show positive self concepts and personal self-esteem.
   b.   Black children show strong to moderate preferences for white images.
   c.   Racial Preference is independent of self esteem in Black children.
   d.   White racial preference is not only a function of race/color theory.

Short Answer

(pp. 40)   1.   Define the Black Self-Hatred Theory.

(pp. 45)   2.   Is the "Black Self-Hatred" thesis an ethnocentric theory? Why or why not?

(pp. 53-54)   3.   Define "black self concept". What are some specific characteristics which form self-conception in African-Americans?

(pp. 43-44)   4.   How do the ethnocentric assumptions negatively affect the "Black Self-Hatred" thesis?

(pp. 41-42)   5.   Define the term "culture" as used in the article. According to the article, how does culture affect the formation of self-concept?

(pp. 41-42)   6.   According to the article, what is the significance of culture?

(pp. 40-41)   7.   According to the article, how would the assumptions of a cultural relativistic perspective differ from the assumptions of "The Black Self-Hatred Paradigm"?

(pp. 43-44)   8.   Name the approach which assumes that one's cultural standards and assumptions are universal?

(pp. 41)   9.   What is the "bicultural" explanation of the "Black Self-Hatred Thesis". How was this explanation developed and what is the main criticism of this analysis?

(pp. 45)   10.   Define Racial Preference Studies.

African-American Gay Youth: One Form of Manhood
Kenneth P. Monteiro and Vincent Faqua

Multiple Choice

(pp. 59-60)   1. According to the article which of the following is cited as issues
                     faced by African-American gay youth?
                     a. facing cultural and racial marginalization
                     b. facing marginalization of their sexuality
                     c. dealing with a deeply conflicted identity
                     d. all of the above

(pp. 59)   2. Which of the following points is **NOT** made in the introduction?
                     a. the gay experience is marginalized in Western culture.
                     b. there is a very small amount of research on African-American gay
                         issues.
                     c. Western psychology has appropriate models to describe and
                         explain the African-American gay experience.
                     d. None of the above.

(pp. 59-60)   3. According to the article, which dimension of sexuality is commonly
                     defined by the term "gay"?
                     a. sexual identity
                     b. sexual actions
                     c. both a and b
                     d. none of the above

(pp. 62-63)   4. The author states that . . .
                     a. the definition of homosexuality differs from culture to culture.
                     b. situational and personal context define the meaning of
                         homosexual acts.
                     c. male to male public intimacy is encouraged in African-American
                         culture.
                     d. all of the above.

(pp. 62-64)   5.   Which of the following is **NOT** cited in the article as characteristics of the African centered approach in describing social experience?
a.   wholistic
b.   materialistic
c.   sees things as simultaneously similar and different
d.   emphasizes the spiritual origin of physical objects in the world

(pp. 62-63)   6.   Which of the following are assumptions of the European framework?
a.   reductionism
b.   empiricism
c.   dualism
d.   all of the above

(pp. 64-65)   7.   According to the article, which statement is **FALSE**? African-American models of psycho sexual experience. . .
a.   are opposite of European models.
b.   reflect the mixed cultural experience of African-Americans.
c.   incorporate elements of European frameworks.
d.   incorporate elements of ancient African philosophy.

(pp. 66)   8.   African-American gay man are **NOT** . . . .
a.   influenced by two antagonistic models of social values and masculinity.
b.   hypermacho, hypersexual, and encouraged to be only sexual initiators .
c.   devalued in a heterosexual White male dominated society.
d.   challenged by a "two-ness" or dual reality in everyday life.

(pp. 66-68)   9.   The African-American model of masculinity. . .
a.   encourages men to be simultaneously assertive and nurturing.
b.   has no values in common with the European model of masculinity.
c.   has no values in common with the European model of femininity.
d.   None of the above

(pp. 67-68)   10.   Which of the following is **UNTRUE?**
The theoretical model of ethnic identity formation in African-Americans . . . .
a.   is a process used to resolve conflicting models of masculinity.
b.   occurs in several stages.
c.   ends with the need to deny all that is European/White
d.   ends with a confident acceptance of African culture.

Short Answers

(pp. 69-70)   1. Discuss the Cass's stage model of homosexual identity formation.

(pp. 69-70)   2. How does the European and African-American gay experience differ?

(pp. 71-72)   3. Describe the gay self-hatred model.

(pp. 74-75)   4. Briefly discus Monteiro's view of what future African-centered research methodologies should emphasize.

(pp. 71-74)   5. According to the author, social maladjustment to race and sexuality is related to what. Discuss briefly.

(pp. 60)   6. What is the relationship between "horseplay" and professional
                      football players?

(pp. 64-65)   7. What is the "paradox" in the African-American community
                      regarding tolerance of homosexuality?

(pp. 68-69)   8. Briefly discuss at least two conflicting positions held by African-
                      American social scientist regarding homosexuality in the African-
                      American community.

(pp. 71-72)   9. What are the criticisms of the gay self-hatred model?

(pp. 65-66)   10. What are the two models of masculinity offered to the African-
                      American male?

African Americans and Reading: A Cognitivist View
Kenneth P. Monteiro

Multiple Choice

(pp. 79)   1. Monteiro takes issue with assumptions underlying the popular
             question "Why can't Johnny read?" for two reasons. Which of
             the following was (were) mentioned as assumptions in the above
             questions:
             a.   that reading problems are limited to boys
             b.   that children now a days truly can not read
             c.   that children who do not read lack the ability to read
             d.   b & c

(pp. 80)   2. The organic deficit models and the socio-cultural deficit models of
             African Americans behavior are similar in that they both postulate:
             a.   an inherent inferiority of African Americans as compared to
                  European
             b.   social and institutional structures
             c.   an inherent superiority of African Americans compared to
                  European Americans
             d.   deficiencies in the genetic make up of African Americans

(pp. 80)   3. The socio-structural models typically focus on
             a.   individual differences
             b.   social and institutional structure
             c.   mental and personality structures
             d.   all the above

(pp. 80)   4. The African and African Americanist models differ from the
             other models of African American behavior in that they
             a.   assume that African American development is normal
             b.   do not compare African Americans to European Americans
             c.   are intended to serve the needs of African Americans
             d.   all of the above

(pp. 82-84)   5. In general studies that looked at phonological and syntactic
             interference between Black English (BE) and Standard English
             (SE) found
             a.   that BE interfered with written SE but not spoken SE
             b.   that BE interfered with spoken SE but not written SE

       c.   that BE interfered with both spoken SE but not written SE

       d.   that BE did not interfere with SE

(pp. 83)   6.   When African American and European American students were given SE and BE versions of a passage they found that

       a.   African Americans performed equally well on both the SE and BE versions

       b.   African Americans performed better than European Americans on the BE versions

       c.   European Americans performed better than African Americans on SE versions

       d.   all of the above

(pp. 85-86)   7.   Jensen and Fredricksen tested African American and European American children on their recall for word lists and so did Franklin and Fulani. They:

       a.   both hypothesized that there were two levels of intellectual functioning

       b.   differed in the Franklin and Fulani found that culture influenced recall

       c.   differed in that Jensen and Fredericksen used lists of words generated from the cultures of both groups.

       d.   all of the above

(pp. 86)   8.   In story comprehension, Reynolds et al. gave African American and European American children a story about two children playing a game involving verbal teasing. The European American children were less likely to recognize this as a story about playing. They hypothesized that the European American children in this study

       a.   happened to be poorer readers than the African American children

       b.   did not have the appropriate schema for reading the story

       c.   were reading the story at a deeper more complex level

       d.   none of the above, the European American children actually outperformed the African American children in their reading comprehension of this story.

(pp. 89-90)   9.   Which of the following reason(s) were given by Monteiro for avoiding the term "under-achievement" when referring to African American literacy.

       a.   In the last 100 years, African Americans have demonstrated much greater increases in the proportion of their population that is literate than have European Americans.

b.   In the last 100 years, African Americans have almost closed the literacy gap between themselves and European Americans even though for the last 50 years there has been no change in the gap between the financial statutes of the two groups.

c.   For virtually all of the history of this country up to the present, African Americans have been afforded inferior educational training.

d.   all of the above

(pp. 94-95)   10.   Which is not a factor that is likely to significantly increase reading comprehension or motivation for African American children:

a.   culturally relevant material

b.   training children to match sounds with the written word

c.   preparing the student with relevant knowledge about the text

d.   teaching the children standard pronunciation of words

Short Answers

(pp. 80-81)   1.   Briefly define the four ideological models concerning the study of African American behavior.

(pp. 81)   2.   Distinguish between surface and deep-structure deficiencies in language performance.

(pp. 82-84)   3.   What was the general finding concerning linguistic interference caused by differences in phonology between BE and SE.

(pp. 84-85)   4.   What is the two level model of intelligence postulated by Jensen
                 and Fredericksen, and how do their results concerning the recall of
                 categorized words relate to this model?

(pp. 85)   5.   What did Franklin and Fulani found in their study of recall of
                 clustered words when word lists were first selected separately
                 from groups of African American and European American students?

(pp. 86-87)   6.   Describe the results of Reynolds et al.'s study of children reading a
                 story about "capping" and Steffensen et al.'s study of students reading
                 about Indian and American weddings. How did they explain these
                 results?

(pp. 87)   7.   In Smith & Lewis's study of young African-American children
                 reading three types of stories, one about European-American
                 characters one about African-American characters and one about
                 animals, what were the basic results and what were the explanations
                 for these results.

(pp. 89-90)   8. What were the patterns in changes of literacy and income for African-Americans and European-Americans over the past century and what do they imply about African-Americans literacy achievement?

(pp. 91)   9. Labov (1982) reported a study of a Philadelphia school district where African-American and European-American children enter with equivalent reading scores and were both groups begin on par with the national average. What happens to each group of students between elementary school and high school, and what are the implications of these changes?

(pp. 93-95)   10. Indicate three suggestions for educators concerning improving reading education of African Americans.

Africanity and the Black Family

Wade W. Nobles

Multiple Choice

(pp. 100)   1. The belief that one's existence is interconnected to the existence of all
              else is:
              a. ontological
              b. cosmological
              c. traditional
              d. Parenthetical

(pp. 103)   2. According to Nobles, the socialization process is like culture because
              it:
              a. influences our preception, knowledge and understanding of social
                  reality
              b. uses abstractness as bases of reality
              c. deals with creating patterns for developing reality
              d. provides patterns for interpreting reality

(pp. 104)   3. "Transubstantive errors" in the study of the Black family in the
              United States are committed by:
              a. Black and White social scientists
              b. Traditional African thinkers
              c. a and b
              d. Anglo-American society

(pp. 102)   4. "Descriptively vitalistic refers to:
              a. The Western concept of time
              b. Empirical time
              c. the concept that time is both rhythmic and stable
              d. b and c

(pp. 107)   5. In terms of the organizational purpose of the Black family, the
              family's reason for being is:
              a. self actualization
              b. kinship ties
              c. childcenteredness
              d. elasticity

(pp. 105-106)   6. The potential for committing the transubstantive error is _____
as one_____ their understanding of the cultural substance
of a particular people.
a.   decreased, increases
b.   increased, decreases
c.   concealed, conceptualizes
d.   controlled, internalizes

(pp. 109-110)   7. Black children are socialized to assume mature responsibilities at an
early age in order to:
a.   reinforce their sense of self worth
b.   help them negotiate the adult world
c.   provide them with practical skills
d.   all the above.

(pp. 110-111)   8. In Nobles' study of the Black family, he found that:
a.   is responsible for the violence in the Black community.
b.   African American had distinctive characteristics of the Traditional
Asian American family
c.   is rooted in the traditional African belief system
d.   is falling apart.

(pp. 110)   9. According to the data on role performance, Black parents feel that
both their male and female children should be equipped with the
_____ _____ and _____ _____
to support themselves and their families as adults.
a.   viable attitudes, flexible mines
b.   psychological attitudes, pragmatic skills
c.   living history, family transitions
d.   distinctive performance, magnetic personalities

(pp. 110)   10. The role of the elderly in the Black family is:
a.   to carry on the family heritage and history
b.   tell stories to the children
c.   instill in the children a sense of family
d.   all the above

Short Answers

(pp. 100)   1. In what way can ones' cultural world view function as blinders?

(pp. 103)   2. Based on the Traditional African belief system, define the concept of
                       space and time.

(pp. 110-111)   3. List two ways in which Traditional African beliefs are rooted in
                       African American Families.

(pp. 100-102)   4. What characterizes African Peoples' understanding of the universe?
                       Discuss briefly.

(pp. 104-105)   5. What is "conceptual incarceration? Give two examples.

(pp. 107-108)   6.   Explain "family networking".

(pp. 109-110)   7.   In what way does the Black family in the US. have flexible and interchangeable roles.

(pp. 103-105)   8.   What should the role of Black Social Scientist be in the analysis of the Black family?

(pp. 100)   9.   According to Nobles, what is the most important criterion of culture?

(pp. 102-103)   10. Explain the notion of self in accordance to the African belief system.

Asian-American Psychology

❖　　　❖　　　❖

Asian American Psychology: A Critical Introduction
Benjamin R. Tong

Multiple Choice

(pp. 119)　　　　1.　The term "Oriental" is an Eurocentric term that assumes:
　　　　a.　Europe is the central standard of measure for all things geo-political
　　　　b.　Orientals are free of all European influences
　　　　c.　Europeans indirectly influence all cultures
　　　　d.　European standards of psychology are appropriate in all situations.

(pp. 119)　　　　2.　According to the author, "Asian-Americans" as a singular, mono culture entity does not exist because:
　　　　a.　they are not truly considered Americans
　　　　b.　the term Asian-American is a Eurocentric term meant to demean Asian-Americans
　　　　c.　each ethnicity in the Asian-American culture is a separate and distinct culture
　　　　d.　the term is radical in nature, and considered dangerous to the "Asian-American movement.

(pp. 120)　　　　3.　The author considers Chin and Chan's interpretation of identity and assimilation as:
　　　　a.　over simplistic and inaccurate
　　　　b.　demeaning and esoteric
　　　　c.　accurate and comprehensive
　　　　d.　easy to follow, understand and accurate.

(pp. 121)　　　　4.　An example of "colonial assimilation" is an Asian-American trying to
　　　　a.　act white by having white friends, or attending a white school
　　　　b.　"colonize" his Asian friends by introducing them to the white culture
　　　　c.　act out the "model minority" myth by acting like a "well

23

behaved, lay low yellow".
d.   gain equal access to political and economic rights and resources guaranteed to the whites

(pp. 122)   5.   What lies at the root of many of the psychological problems of Asian-Americans?
a.   racism
b.   lack of adequate housing
c.   the individualistic culture of Asian-Americans.
d.   lack of education

(pp. 121)   6.   An example of "egalitarian assimilation" is an Asian American who:
a.   insists on equal access to political and economic rights and resources guaranteed to whites.
b.   insists on equal rights for males and females
c.   believes that children of Asian-Americans should be given the same rights as adults.
d.   must be accepted by the Whites.

(pp. 117-118)   7.   Psychiatrist Keh-ming Lin discovered that the anti psychotic drug holoperidol and the anti anxiety drug alprazolam
a.   metabolized faster in Asian-Americans than in Whites
b.   did not metabolize as well in Asian-Americans as in Whites
c.   metabolized slower in Asian-Americans than in Whites
d.   are widely available on nonprescription basis

(pp. 120)   8.   Tong suggests that in terms of the psychology of identity and assimilation, there exists
a.   assimilated versus unassimilated Asian-Americans.
b.   imitation whites versus perpetual exotic liens.
c.   bicultural types
d.   types and modes of participation.

(pp. 119-120)   9.   With respect to "Yellow America", literal assimilation is connected with those Asian-Americans with mindsets and personalities best represented by which behavior?
a.   Asian-Americans trying to "pass" for White
b.   Asian-Americans living only for White acceptance, the stereotype "model minority"
c.   Asian-Americans insisting on equal access to political and economic rights and resources.
d.   Asian-Americans who believe in the Freudian Interpretation of life.

(pp. 119-120)   10.   Approximately 43% of a total of 7.5 million Asian-American live
  a.   below the poverty line
  b.   in politically correct neighborhoods
  c.   in colonized neighborhoods
  d.   none of the above

Short Answers

(pp. 117-122)   1.   What are some of the results of the "model minority" myth on the Asian American culture?

(pp. 122)   2.   According to the author, what is "collective racist trauma?"

(pp. 122)   3.   Why does the author not like the term "assimilation?"

(pp. 117)   4.   What was one of the earlier assumptions of Western Psychology?

(pp. 117-122)   5.   Compare and contrast the three types of assimilation?

(pp. 117-122)   6.   Briefly discuss collective racist trauma.

(pp. 117-122)   7.   Briefly name describe three modes of participation associated with
the three types of assimilation.

(pp. 117-122)   8.   According to Tong, what are the A-B-C's of the human condition?

(pp. 117-122)   9.   Discuss briefly, the faulty assumption made by the "great
White father of American journalism and social journalism".

(pp. 117-122)   10.   In terms of collective racist trauma, what discuss briefly the events
that has affected the Filipino, Japanese and Vietnamese American
people.

The Transgenerational Impact of the Japanese American Internment: Clinical Issues in Working with the Children of Former Internees.

Donna K. Nagata

Multiple Choice

(pp. 127)   1. The Nisei felt especially victimized by the internment experience because:
   a.   they were subject to taunting by real Americans
   b.   America was their country of citizenship and they felt rejected because of the internment
   c.   they were beaten and robbed during the internment
   d.   their camps did not have the luxuries of home.

(pp. 127)   2. According to the author, Japanese Americans who served in internment camps:
   a.   talk freely about their camp experiences with anyone
   b.   look at their camp experience as crucial to their development as individuals
   c.   rarely talk about their internment experiences with their family
   d.   were bitter because they were not allowed to fight during the war.

(pp. 128)   3. What is one indicator that a Sansei may be the child of a former internee?
   a.   the Sansei usually will have an identifying tattoo
   b.   the Sansei usually feels a close bond with all family members, including those who were interned
   c.   Family communication is inhibited
   d.   Communication between family members is relaxed and educational

(pp. 127)   4. Interviews conducted Nagata suggest the internment of the Nisei has:
   a.   had no effect of their children
   b.   been an educational experience
   c.   shaped the lives of their children
   d.   shown that internment served its purpose by preventing the Japanese from overthrowing the American Government.

(pp. 127)   5. According to the Author, as a result of the internment camp, some
                   Niseis and some Sanseis experienced:
                   a. problems of low self esteem, after perceiving to have failed to
                       prove their self worth to their nation
                   b. a new need to explore the land in which they were interned
                   c. problems of reapplying for citizenship
                   d. joy and happiness that their years of internment were over

(pp. 130-131) 6. Nagata notes that some Sansei may have chosen a career as a
                   lawyer in order to:
                   a. recover financial losses incurred by their parents during World
                       War II.
                   b. dispel the stereotype that Japanese are passive
                   c. utilize a form of empowerment, and to prevent anything similar to
                       the internment experience from occurring again
                   d. to file class action law suit against the United States Government
                       for civil rights abuse.

(pp. 128-132) 7. Some issues that need to be explored during therapy with the Sansei
                   generation include:
                   a. issues of identity, assertiveness, vocational choices, self-esteem
                       and family communication
                   b. issues of self humor and psycho-social repression on their
                       socio-economic status
                   c. their role in American Society
                   d. their Freudian tendency to assimilate into a psycho-sexual
                       revolution

(pp. 129-130) 8. During treatment with Sanseis the therapist will usually find the
                   issue of internment:
                   a. antagonistic to the ideals of Freudian psychology
                   b. not occur as explicit problems among the Sansei clients
                   c. a subject that is neglected because it has no historical
                       significance
                   d. resolved, as a result of the restitution paid to the internees.

(pp. 133-134) 9. During treatment, a useful method of narrative therapy as
                   introduced by Polkinghorne includes the "what if" narratives, an
                   example of this would be:
                   a. during therapy repeating what if, until the patient discovers what
                       really is
                   b. construct hypothetical scenarios relating to internment that can

help express their grief and to understand the impact of internment on their experience
c. creating a hierarchy of "what if" fear and placing internment on the top of the hierarchy
d. exploring the indecisiveness that is typical of the Sansei generation

(pp. 134-135) 10. Why does the author believe the presence of a Japanese American therapist is helpful during therapy with most Sansei clients?
a. they share similar culture, social history, and are usually easier to develop trust with
b. their in-depth knowledge of Freudian psychology is an invaluable aid to therapy
c. their rates are generally cheaper than that of a White therapist
d. they often find the Japanese American therapist extremely valuable for their translation skills.

Short Answers

(pp. 128) 1. Why would some of the Japanese-American be reluctant to talk about their experiences as internees?

(pp. 128-129) 2. How prevalent are and what type of effects did internment have on the Sansei generation?

(pp. 127) 3. The author cites the quotation (with respect to the Holocaust) "the more profound the outer silence, the more pervasive was the inner impact of the events." How can you relate this to the Japanese Internment experience?

(pp. 128)   4.   According to the author what would be one of the first problems faced by a therapist when treating a Sansei?

(pp. 129-130)   5.   How is the issue of self esteem related to the issue of internment?

(pp. 130-131)   6.   What are some of the positive effects the internment might have had on the vocational choices of the Sanseis?

(pp. 132-133)   7.   What are some of the shortcomings of family therapy?

(pp. 132-133)   8.   What are some of the advantages of Narrative Therapy?

(pp. 134-135)   9.   How would you summarize the authors perspective on the type of therapist that would be most effective for a Sansei client?

(pp. 135-136)   10.   What are some of the factors that determine how a client will respond to therapy?

An Analysis of Domestic Violence in Asian American Communities: A Multiculture Approach to Counseling
Christine K. Ho

Multiple Choice

(pp. 139) 1. The author believes that when applied to the Asian American community, current models of domestic violence which are based on analysis of Western society are:
a. adequate models from which to offer diagnosis
b. adequate models from which to build a new theory of Asian American psychology
c. dynamic in scope, relevancy, and of indispensable value to the therapist
d. inadequate, because it addresses the problems from a Western perspective

(pp. 140-141) 2. According to the author, Asian American culture stress:
a. autonomy and independence
b. total respect of Buddhism
c. complete and total dedication to the Western lifestyle
d. orientation toward the family, hierarchy, and order

(pp. 142) 3. Binding the foot of the female in the Chinese culture serves to:
a. save the family money in the cost of buying shoes.
b. save the face of the family
c. encourage domestic violence by preventing the female from running away
d. foster dependence, helplessness and immobility in the women

(pp. 144) 4. One form of covert racism in Western culture listed in this article is:
a. Belief that the Western approach to therapy is effective for all cultural background
b. the beating of Vincent Chin
c. World War II internment camps
d. rejecting applicants to Harvard because they are Asian

(pp. 146-147) 5. In the focus group conducted in this article, Chinese women viewed domestic violence as:
    a. an unacceptable way of life
    b. permissible under Confucian tradition
    c. in accordance with Buddhist philosophy
    d. a way to restore filial piety after the Chinese Exclusion Act.

(pp. 141) 6. Chinese American women feel that it is inappropriate to get help outside the family in cases of domestic violence because:
    a. it would bring shame to the family
    b. the husband would be put in jail
    c. the problems can be solved by the husband and wife
    d. the wife would be blamed for the problem

(pp. 144-145) 7. According to the author, many Asian Americans look at the Western legal system with:
    a. distrust and dislike
    b. awe and amazement
    c. open arms for its interest in justice
    d. a system in need of reform

(pp. 144) 8. In contrast to the views of other Southeast Asian groups, the Chinese generally feel that physical violence is:
    a. less openly accepted
    b. advocated by Buddhist teaching
    c. openly accepted
    d. an effective way of educating the children

(pp. 148) 9. Which of the following is most likely to occur when police intervene in Asian American domestic violence cases:
    a. further violence may be inhibited because of the guilt and shame aroused by public exposure
    b. violence will increased because of the shame brought upon the family
    c. Asian Americans are likely to join the police force
    d. the husband will be put in jail.

(pp. 150-151) 10. The author suggest that women can gain the rights against physical abuse by:
    a. continuing research in the area of Western domestic violence
    b. forming political action committees whose purpose is to address the issues of domestic violence

       c.   challenging the status of unequal power of men and women in the Asian American communities

       d.   fighting violence with violence

Short Answers

(pp. 138-139)   1.   What may account for the relatively low reporting rate of domestic violence by Asian American families?

(pp. 141)   2.   What are some of the negative effects of "filial piety" within the Asian American families?

(pp. 142)   3.   Briefly discuss how an Asian American woman who follows the philosophies that influence Asian countries, would view domestic violence?

(pp. 143)   4.   Discuss some of the factors that may discourage Asian American women from changing their inferior and oppressive positions?

(pp. 145-146)   5.   Compare and contrast Chinese and Vietnamese husbands' views of their spouses.

(pp. 147-148)   6.   According to the study in this article, what were some Asian American women's viewpoints on domestic violence?

(pp. 147)   7.   Why are many Asian American women reluctant to leave battered relationships?

(pp. 144)   8.   Discuss briefly why domestic violence among immigrant and refugee populations is a more complex problem than among second and third generation Asian Americans.

(pp. 148-149)   9.   List and discuss some of the issues that therapist need to explore when treating Asian American women living with domestic violence?

(pp. 149-151)   10.   What are the methods propose by Christine Ho to address the issue of domestic violence in Asian American communities?

Death and Dying: A Vietnamese Cultural Perspective
Chuong Chung

Multiple Choice

(pp. 153)   1.   According to the author, the treatment of Vietnamese patients is
                     difficult due to both the language barrier as well as:
                     a.   their inclination to reveal every detail of their trauma
                     b.   the lack of detail provided and a resistance to revealing feelings
                          and emotions
                     c.   a tendency to wait up to three months before discussing a
                          traumatic event
                     d.   both b and c

(pp. 153)   2.   Two societies which have greatly influenced Vietnamese tradition and
                     culture are:
                     a.   India and China
                     b.   China and France
                     c.   United States and China
                     d.   United States and France

(pp. 154-155)   3.   Central to the Vietnamese belief system are the "The Three
                     Religions" which include:
                     a.   Toaism, Christianity, and Buddhism
                     b.   Baptist, Confucianism, and Toaism
                     c.   Buddhism, Confucianism, and Taoism
                     d.   Episcopalian, Taoism, and Buddhism

(pp. 155-156)   4.   According to Confucianism, regulation and good order of the three
                     levels of existence (ie: person, family, and nation) were proof that
                     universal harmony prevailed. The way to maintain this harmony was
                     through:
                     a.   ceremonial sacrifices and libations
                     b.   fulfillment of all obligations
                     c.   ancestor worship
                     d.   none of the above

(pp. 156-157)   5.   Which of the following is NOT one of the four Noble Truths
                     taught by Buddhism?
                     a.   follow the Eight fold Path
                     b.   suffering is caused by inherently insatiable desires

    c.   desires must be indulged in as a way to end suffering and existence

    d.   existence is suffering

(pp. 158)   6. Which is NOT an aspect of "ancestor worship?"

    a.   commemoration of the anniversary of an ancestor's death

    b.   visiting and caring for the tombs of the deceased

    c.   offering of food and drink and prayers said to the ancestor altar

    d.   none of the above - all are aspects of ancestor worship

(pp. 158-159)   7. Despite recent efforts to understand how Vietnamese Americans cope with stress, there is still very little known about how this culture deals with death, grief, and:

    a.   terminal illness

    b.   natural disasters

    c.   bereavement

    d.   both a and c

(pp. 160)   8. The way in which Vietnamese Americans cope with the stress of having lost a loved one is by:

    a.   expressing their grief verbally to a Psychologist

    b.   providing to the deceased all the rituals and services according to the family's religious affiliation

    c.   throwing the ashes of the deceased into the nearest river as an offering to the Gods

    d.   attending groups where close friends gather and exchange stories remembering the deceased

(pp. 160)   9. The Vietnamese "khuyen lon" or "an ui" (consoling), is similar to the Western counseling approach in that it tells a grieving family member that:

    a.   it's not their fault

    b.   they must face their loss by getting back to their regular routine

    c.   only time will heal their pain

    d.   both b and c

(pp. 161)   10. According to the authors, what does this article aim to do?

    a.   contribute to the development of cross-cultural approaches to diagnosis and treatment

    b.   provide useful information to professionals so they may better serve the Vietnamese-American population

    c.   help produce clinicians who are both empathic and

flexible to cross-cultural perspectives

d.   all of the above

Short Answers

(pp. 152-161)   1.   Name a consequence of the lack of literature describing the way the Vietnamese cope with death and the stress of losing a loved one?

(pp. 152-161)   2.   What are the two main attempts of this article as stated by the author?

(pp. 152-161)   3.   How have foreign influences contributed to cultural changes among the Vietnamese?

(pp. 152-161)   4.   What constitutes the complex cultural profile of the Vietnamese now living in America?

(pp. 152-161)   5.   What does the text say about "Humanism?" What is its role in Vietnamese culture?

(pp. 155-156)   6.   What are the "Three Religions?" What is their significance in
                        Vietnamese culture?

(pp. 155-156)   7.   Briefly describe the practice of "ancestor worship."

                   8.   Why is it important that a deceased relative be honored with funeral
                        rites?

(pp. 157)   9.   Why is it difficult to paint a cultural profile of the "typical"
                        Vietnamese?

(pp. 160-161)   10.   How do the Vietnamese view sadness and grief? How does this view
                        contrast with the one held by Western cultures?

Chinese American Culture: Still Paradigmatically Crazy After All These Years

Benjamin R. Tong

Multiple Choice

(pp. 167-168)   1.   Why does the author quote Harvard doctoral student Jean Wu?
   a.   as a Chinese American, she is well aware of the true nature of being Chinese in America
   b.   she is an example of a Chinese American who probably has been affected by Imperial Confucianism doctrine and the institutional racism of white dominated America.
   c.   her dissertation addresses the problems of being Chinese in America
   d.   as a minority who does modeling for Macy's and a Harvard doctoral student, she is truly the model minority.

(pp. 162-163)   2.   The author sees Ronald Takaki and his "Strangers from a Different Shore" as:
   a.   a valuable source of insight into the Chinese-American culture
   b.   an ambitious yet ignorant piece of work concerning Chinese-American culture
   c.   a literary work comparable to that of Maxine Hong Kingston's "Woman Warrior," and "Chinamen" both of which explore mythology, legends, sexism, and racism.
   d.   an example of an author who fails to address the topic of the Chinese-American culture

(pp. 163-164)   3.   The author realizes the type of influence a best selling author like Maxine Hong Kingston can have on the publics perception of Chinese American culture, the author sees Maxine's work as:
   a.   an example of a Chinese-American writer who overcame racism and then used her best selling books to accurately portray the life of a typical Chinese-American woman.
   b.   a writer whose feminist books are at the forefront of accurately identifying some of the issues that need to be raised in the study of Chinese-American culture.
   c.   a bad omen, because as best selling novels her works have had a profound effect on the publics perception of Chinese-American culture, unfortunately the novels present Chinese America as unnecessarily "mythic", and the Chinese-American men

as misogynistic and unfaithful to tradition.

d. an example of the type of work that need not succumb to the traditional norms of American Literature to become a best seller, does this by accurately exploring the new mythology of the Chinese-American culture.

(pp. 163-164) 4. The "either -or" paradigm of viewing Chinese-American culture, introduced to us by Jeff Chan and Frank Chin is viewed by the author as:

a. either a very good perspective of viewing Chinese-American culture of an inadequate perspective of viewing Chinese-American culture, depending on your own idiosyncratic views.

b. the incorrect perspective of viewing Chinese-American culture because it introduces the idea that the Chinese-American culture is one that can be either the perfect model minority or the Asian-American with a complete history, literature, language, mythology and sensibility all their own.

c. the correct perspective of viewing Asian-American culture because it allows the concept of "either-or", while being abstract, to empirically compare the Asian-American culture to either the American (white ways) style or the Traditional Chinese style leading to a clear and accurate understanding of Chinese-American culture.

d. an incorrect perspective on viewing Chinese-American culture because it proposes that the Chinese in America are a race of people who are foreigners and do not belong in America, or a race of people who can only imitate the American way of life reserved only for White people.

(pp. 163-164) 5. How does the author view the idea of "model minority" as introduced through the "either-or" framework of Jeffrey Chan and Frank Chin?

a. a "True Gold Mine" for Chinese American's who carry physical features that America finds attractive, and thus will have very successful careers as models.

b. a point of view that accurately depicts the struggle of Chinese-Americans, and should be included in any paradigm that seeks to understand the Chinese-American culture.

c. a corollary of the "either-or" paradigm that fails to adequately address the true problem in studying the Asian American culture.

d. a psychological phenomenon that occurs exclusively in the Chinese-American culture, because they are so in need of aligning their behavior to their model majority status.

(pp. 167)   6. The author would agree with which of the following statements
                  in regards to Chinese-American culture?
              a. Chinese-American culture is alive, constantly changing, and its
                  variations can never truly be enumerated.
              b. Chinese-American culture should seek to conform to the
                  American way of life because it would legitimize their roles as
                  Americans.
              c. the Chinese in America should learn to read and write in the
                  classical Chinese text, since 55 percent of the population between
                  the ages of 15 and 25 in China cannot read or write the classical
                  Chinese text.
              d. the existence of a Chinese-American culture is nothing but a
                  patchwork of psychological and cultural perplexity seeking to be
                  legitimized in American culture.

(pp. 165-166) 7. What is the "three dimensional" paradigm?
              a. the model proposed by the author as a conceptual framework
                  from which to study Chinese-American culture.
              b. the necessary component needed for Chinese-Americans to be a
                  model in today's cosmopolitan world.
              c. the true personality of the Chinese-American, the three
                  dimensional paradigm includes the docility, humbleness, and
                  passivity that is inherent in all Chinese.
              d. a frame of reference for viewing Chinese-American Culture
                  advocated by Dr. Stanley Sue.

(pp. 165-166) 8. What is so significant about the "three dimensional" paradigm?
              a. it is offered as an analogy, comparing the advanced technology
                  found in today's world with many of the cultural advances that
                  have been studied regarding Chinese-American culture.
              b. it finally gives credit to the Chinese-American who invented
                  "three dimensional" technology and is a tribute to the stereotype
                  that the Chinese are either well educated and docile or both.
              c. It is a conceptual framework introduced to us by the author as a
                  paradigm that seeks to understand Chinese-American culture by
                  bringing to light the origins, the nature, and the consequences of
                  Chinese-American culture.
              d. it's significance can be found in the fact that it confirms the
                  idealism of the Chinese-American culture as an eclectic mix of
                  Confucianism, Taoism, and Buddhism.

(pp. 165-166)   9.   In trying to study Chinese American culture, which of the following methods would the author recommend as producing research that could adequately explain Chinese American Culture?
   a.   a background search into the "model minority" myth , most importantly it's origins and it's validity concerning Chinese American culture.
   b.   an extensive research into Confucianism, Taoism, and Buddhism and why it is rejected by many of the Chinese Americans youths of today.
   c.   a perusal through the works of Maxine Hong Kingston, Ronald Takaki, Jeffrey Chan and Frank Chin, with each source offering an authoritative and accurate view of Chinese American culture.
   d.   an examination of cultural aspects that are transplanted and transformed from Chinese culture, as well as investigation of the unique experiences from the American life.

(pp. 165-166)   10.   Of the following items, which would the author most agree as exemplifying the "transplanted" model of the "three dimensional paradigm"?
   a.   The practice of eating fortune cookies after dinner, a tradition that finds it's origins in Chinese American culture.
   b.   Harvard doctoral student Jean Wu's comment concerning her views on Chinese American culture and her statement "To be successful in America, especially if you're Asian , you have to learn to be somebody not yourself . . . it's all aggression and competition."
   c.   A model minority student going over his engineering text studying for exams as if preparing for the traditional exams reserved for scholars in China.
   d.   In America, the practice of displaying statues such as Guan Gwng, a tradition which finds its roots from old world Chinese culture.

Short Answers

(pp. 167-168)   1.   Of the two, imperial or classical Confucianism, which does the author believe has had a more profound influence on Chinese-American culture?

(pp. 168)   2. In regards to Chinese-American culture, what role does the author
                     believe Imperial Confucianism has had on the Chinese in America?

(pp. 168)   3. Why does the author quote Dr. Stanley Sue and Harvard doctoral
                     student Jean Wu?

(pp. 163-168)   4. The author mentions "The Woman Warrior", by Maxine Hong
                     Kingston, in the beginning of his article, and mentions the woman
                     warrior again near the end of the article. Compare or contrast the
                     author's perspective on the two.

(pp. 168-169)   5. Does Tong feel Classical Confucianism should have a broader
                     influence on Chinese-American culture? Why or why not?

(pp. 162-163)   6. Explain what Tong means by the statement that Chinese Americans
                     are not "Chinese"?

(pp. 163-164)   7.   Discuss the three major positions taken in literature concerning Chinese American culture?

(pp. 163-164)   8.   Discuss the "either-or" view, as proposed by Jeffrey Chan and Frank Chin, what are some of the consequences?

(pp. 165-166)   9.   What does Tong suggest as ways of better understanding the Chinese American culture?

(pp. 168)   10.   Using the "three dimensional" paradigm, what is Tong's conclusion concerning Chinese American culture

Chicano-/Latino- Psychology

❖   ❖   ❖

Synopsis of the History of Chicano Psychology
Amado Padilla

Multiple Choice

(pp. 179)   1. Padilla begins by describing Chicano psychology as:
a.   the way Chicanos think and behave
b.   a projection of mainstream American psychology
c.   a part of a larger area called ethnopsychology
d.   a psychosocial paradigm

(pp. 179-180)   2. Chicano psychology emerged:
a.   in Mexico in the early 1950's
b.   as a reaction to stereotypes arrived at by majority group psychologists
c.   as a reaction to intracultural reset in Europe
d.   at a conference in Washington DC in 1979

(pp. 179)   3. Early Chicano psychologists were principally concerned with all of the following except:
a.   intelligence and academic achievement
b.   family life style and its effects on personality
c.   the negative neurological effects of bilingualism
d.   the mental health status of Chicanos

(pp. 179-180)   4. Different writers/historians have alternately named _____ and _____ as "the cradle of psychiatry".
a.   Spain, England
b.   Mexico, France
c.   Spain, Mexico
d.   none of the above

(pp. 184-185)   5. Mexico's *curanderismo* may be accurately described as:
a.   a form of folk medicine practiced by indigenous healers

b. an ethnomedical belief system
c. at least 400 years old
d. all of the above

(pp. 188)   6. Which of the following statements regarding Sanchez, the father of Chicano psychology, is not true:
a. he argued that standardized intelligence tests are invalid when used with Chicano children
b. he founded the Association of Psychologists por la Raza (APLR)
c. he championed the cause of bilingualism
d. he may also be considered the father of Chicano studies

(pp. 189-190)   7. Ruiz' study found that _____ of the total APA membership for 1970 was of Spanish-surnamed origin.
a. a surprisingly large proportion
b. about 10%
c. only 3%
d. less than 1%

(pp. 192-193)   8. Of those Chicano psychologists mentioned:
a. none were specifically trained in the area of Chicano psychology
b. all have served as chairpersons of the APLR
c. all were formally trained in Mexico
d. none were official members of the American Psychological Association (APA).

(pp. 179)   9. Martinez cites all of the following as reasons justifying the idea of Chicano psychology except
a. it is appropriate to study the behavior of Chicanos within that same cultural milieu
b. studies of acculturation may be contained within that rubric
c. simple self defense
d. it is the newest branch of general psychology

(pp. 179-180)   10. The concept that there are local principles of behavior only true with a given culture is a(n) _____ perspective.
a. etic
b. localized
c. emic
d. cultural

Short Answers

(pp. 181-182)   1.   What historic event occurred in 1409, in Spain and why is it significant?

(pp. 183-184)   2.   The Aztecs recognized a variety of mental illnesses and conditions that resemble those treated by modern day psychologists. Describe the similarities between these two perspectives.

(pp. 183-186)   3.   Some scholars would call curandismo an outdated folk belief system. Why do you think the author took the time to discuss this belief system?

(pp. 184-185)   4.   Briefly describe how the Aztecs used principles of taste aversion conditioning to treat alcoholism.

(pp. 186-187)   5.   Summarize the contributions of Ezequiel Chavez to psychology in Mexico.

(pp. 187-188)   6. Which Chicano psychologist wrote about intelligence testing and what was his/her viewpoint?

(pp. 188-189)   7. List the diverse topics that Alfredo Castaneda worked on during the course of his career.

(pp. 190-191)   8. What was the historical significance of the 1971 symposium held in Washington, DC?

(pp. 189-190)   9. What were the theoretical arguments of "Pride and Prejudice: A Mexican American Dilemma"?

(pp. 191-192)   10. How has COSSMHO affected the role of Chicanos in psychology?

Child Bilingualism: The Same Old Issues Revisited

Amado Padilla and Kathryn J. Lindholm

Multiple Choice

(pp. 194)   1. The differing opinions concerning bilingualism are;
    a.   all quite reasonable and can be synthesized
    b.   often held in spite and abundant research
    c.   based on research that begin in the 1960's
    d.   basically the same

(pp. 194-195)   2. The research reviewed in this article is confined almost exclusively to
    a.   adults
    b.   mental patients
    c.   Chicanos
    d.   monolinguals

(pp. 196-197)   3. Language assessment measures overwhelmingly examine aspects of linguistic structure separate from
    a.   word usage
    b.   number of languages spoken
    c.   syntax
    d.   social context

(pp. 204-205)   4. Studies indicate no differences in language development between monolingual and _____ bilingual children.
    a.   simultaneous
    b.   successive
    c.   acquisition
    d.   above average

(pp. 208)   5. Most studies report that bilingual children acquire the rules of each language:
    a.   in a single complex rule structure
    b.   as cognitive matrix
    c.   calibrationally
    d.   separately

(pp. 208-209)   6. Language mixing in bilinguals seems to occur predominantly at the
_____ level.
a.   phonological
b.   morphosyntactic
c.   lexical
d.   subcortical

(pp. 214)   7. Laosa found that differences in the teaching strategies of Chicano
and Anglo mothers_____when he controlled for the
mother's level of formal education.
a.   increased
b.   disappeared
c.   differentiated
d.   remained constant

(pp. 216-217)   8. Bilingual children may be more predisposed to separate word from
referent, and thus arrive earlier at the ability to use language _____
a.   in the home
b.   in school
c.   concretely
d.   symbolically

(pp. 220-221)   9. _____ is the hypothesis that the meaning of words are
made up of smaller arts (features or components of meaning) and
that children learn the meaning of words by gradually adding
features to the terms.
a.   feature assimilation hypothesis
b.   sematic feature hypothesis
c.   phonological loop hypothesis
d.   term-feature coding theory

(pp. 223-225)   10. This article addressed all of the following **EXCEPT:**
a.   strategies for bilingual education
b.   defining and measuring bilingualism
c.   the process of bilingual language development
d.   environmental language input

Short Answers

(pp. 194)   1.   Briefly discuss the relationship between the findings of research and commonly held opinions of bilingualism.

(pp. 196-197)   2.   What are some of the problems common to all three measures in Table 1.

(pp. 200-201)   3.   Define simultaneous and successive bilingualism.

(pp. 208-209)   4.   Discuss briefly, the concepts of transfer and interferences as they relate to bilingual development in children.

(pp. 210-211)   5.   Why might "Spanglish" be considered the norm in some communities?

(pp. 211-212)   6.   How do the sources of language input for Spanish and English differ for 1st generation and 3rd generation Chicanos?

(pp. 215-216)   7.   How does Harris and Hassemer suggest educators should address bilingual children?

(pp. 216-225)   8.   On the basis of the theories of Piaget, Vygotsky, and Leopold, how might bilingual development facilitate cognitive functioning?

(pp. 201-202)   9.   Summarize Ben-Zee's theory that redefined the concept of interference.

(pp. 194-225)   10.   What are the biases mentioned at the beginning of this article?

Spirituality and Family Dynamics in Psychotherapy with Latino Children

Joseph M. Cervantes and Oscar Ramirez

Multiple Choice

(pp. 228-229)   1. The author describes spirituality as a transcendent level of consciousness that allows for existential purpose and mission, the search for harmony and wholeness, and:
   a. an understanding for one's place in life
   b. a fundamental belief in the existence of a greater, all-loving presence in the universe
   c. a belief in the sacredness of nature
   d. an interconnection between man and nature

(pp. 229)   2. "Mestizoization" can best be described as:
   a. the process of acculturation
   b. one culture abandoning their beliefs and converting to the beliefs of another culture
   c. assimilation of one culture to another culture
   d. assimilation of two cultures to each other's beliefs and values

(pp. 232)   3. Which of the following would not be considered an aspect of mestizo spirituality?
   a. individuality
   b. harmony
   c. interdependence
   d. respect for the sacredness of one's place in the world

(pp. 233)   4. The case history of Juan, the ten-year old having difficulties with "witchcraft" illustrates _____ as a paradigm for therapeutic intervention.
   a. social belief systems
   b. religious belief systems
   c. cultural belief systems
   d. familial belief systems

(pp. 235-236)   5. The basic concept of curanderismo is the idea that:
   a. mind and body are distinctly separate
   b. the psychology of the mind is separate from the biology of the mind

      c.   life is holistic, with no artificial boundaries between the mind and body

      d.   health and illness are concepts dealt with by the mind only

(pp. 235-237)   6. Which of the following is not one of the four views of illness and health?

      a.   life is ordained by divine will, namely, the individual's thoughts, intentions, and behavior must be oriented around good deeds

      b.   illness is perceived as a social interpersonal matrix rather than just a chance biological event

      c.   supernatural causes play a major role in both health and illness

      d.   health is viewed as a strictly biological process (in part)

(pp. 237)   7. As an agent of healing, the curandero/curandera uses _____ to provide internal contextual rapport that begins the healing process.

      a.   therapeutic conditioning

      b.   therapeutic imagery

      c.   therapeutic intervention

      d.   therapeutic homeostasis

(pp. 229-230)   8. In dealing with Mexican American families, the author would agree that there is a paradigm shift from:

      a.   the psychology of the family/community to a psychology of the self

      b.   the psychology of the self to a psychology of the family/community

      c.   the psychology of the family/community to a psychology of the culture

      d.   the psychology of the self to mysticism

(pp. 229-230)   9. The mestizo perspective evolved with the following characteristics **EXCEPT**:

      a.   Harmony with the physical and social environment

      b.   An openness to diversity

      c.   A belief in a theistic cosmology that protects, influences and engages all life.

      d   An interconnectedness of psychology and biology

(pp. 241-242) 10. Concerning the treatment of Mexican Americans by family therapists which of the following would the author **NOT** agree with? The therapist must:

      a.   appreciate and learn the Mestizo perspective

    b.   explore the religious and spiritual beliefs of a particular family

    c.   assess how a child has conceptualized balance and harmony in his or her family

    d.   emphasize the inherent separation of spirituality and mental processes.

Short Answers

(pp. 229)   1. Explain the process of "mestizoization."

(pp. 230)   2. Name three of the basic family themes emphasized for children growing up in Mexican-American households.

(pp. 235-236)   3. Define the term *curanderismo*.

(pp. 235-236)   4. In discussing curanderismo, the author mentions four view of illness and health. Briefly describe each view.

(pp. 237)   5. In the role of the philosophy of curanderismo, the author compares the curandero/curandera to the family therapist. Discuss a few of the points he made in this comparison?

(pp. 230)   6. What is the main emphasis of mestizo spirituality?

(pp. 233)   7. In the case of the ten-year old child Juan, how does the family therapist use religious belief systems to assist him and his mother?

(pp. 241-242)   8. In the treatment of Mexican-American families, the author mentions several factors which must be taken into account by the family therapist. Name three.

(pp. 232)   9. Briefly discuss Mestizo spirituality?

(pp. 235-236)   10.   What is the basic concept of Curanderismo?

The Psychological Experience of Puerto Rican Women at Work

Alba N. Rivera-Ramos

Multiple Choice

(pp. 245-246)   1.   In order to improve women's socioeconomic status and achieve economic growth and development, the author suggests there be a change in:

a.   traditional attitudes in which the White-Anglo Saxon Protestant Male is the best model to copy and Hispanic women are the inferior part of humankind.

b.   the role of the employer, in which the employer accepts the fact that he/she is equal to the employee.

c.   the perceived social status of the homemaker

d.   economic enterprises and agencies by implementing social service programs aimed toward women in the workplace.

(pp. 247-248)   2.   In her study examining Puerto Rican women's attitudes and perceptions, River-Ramos found that Puerto Rican women perceived the average Puerto Rican female as:

a.   assertive and liberal

b.   independent and self-sufficient

c.   passive and docile

d.   conservative and traditional

(pp. 248-249)   3.   Rivera-Ramos observed a difference in women's attributions of themselves as individuals and their attributions of the general population of Puerto Rican women. One of the main reasons for this difference is because:

a.   Puerto Rican women have been conditioned to be conservative yet liberal by society.

b.   Puerto Rican women have internalized the ideology of inferiority to the WASPM model.

c.   of the stereotypes of Puerto Rican women as "out to take away men's jobs."

d.   Puerto Rican women, in general, see themselves as passive but see other Puerto Rican women as liberal and independent

(pp. 246-247) 4. Which group of women are considered the most liberal according to the study conducted by Rivera-Ramos (Table 11.1):
a. homemakers
b. professionals
c. students
d. workers

(pp. 249-250) 5. In the study examining prejudice and discrimination against women in the work place:
a. Dark-skinned women were perceived to be just as productive as men.
b. Females looked upon divorced women positively while men looked upon divorced women negatively, as compared to married women.
c. light-skinned women were perceived to be just as productive as men.
d. neither men nor women expressed any form of prejudice towards dark-skinned or divorced women.

(pp. 251) 6. What are the three ways in which environmental stress affects men and women?
a. physiologically, Affectively, and Behaviorally.
b. psychologically, Physiologically, and Conditionally
c. psychologically, Affectively, and Behaviorally
d. physiologically, Behaviorally, and Conditionally

(pp. 252-253) 7. In studying the differences of job-related stress among men and women, which group reported more stress than any of the other groups?
a. unionized men manifested more stress than any other group
b. unionized women manifested more stress than any other group
c. non-unionized men manifested more stress that any other group
d. non-unionized women manifested more stress than any other group

(pp. 252-253) 8. Rivera-Ramos' results on job-related stress found that stress from work affects family life in many ways. Which of the following would not apply to her findings?
a. deterioration in communication with spouse
b. decreased irritability when facing problems of children
c. deterioration in communication with friends and other family members
d. deterioration in self-esteem

(pp. 253-254)   9.   An example of internal social control would be _____ , while
_____would be an example of external social control.
a.   education and mass media; prejudice and discrimination
b.   prejudice and discrimination; education and mass media
c.   education and prejudice; mass media and discrimination
d.   prejudice and mass media; education and discrimination

(pp. 253-255)   10.   To fight the inequalities and rights violations of women in the
workplace, the author makes several recommendations. Which of
the following do not belong?
a.   the organization of self-help groups among Puerto Rican women
b.   programs directed toward the understanding and control of
personal variables (cognitions, affection, and social perception).
c.   a workshop on improving communication with family and friends
d.   the implementation of workshops for supervisors, managers, and
entrepreneurs, directed toward the consideration of the cost
involved in prejudiced and discriminatory practices toward Puerto
Rican women in their recruitment and managerial activities.

Short Answers

(pp. 246-247)   1.   In Rivera-Ramos' study on attitudes and perception, the sample was
categorized into what three main groups?

(pp. 248-249)   2.   The author discusses the gap between Puerto Rican women's
attributions made to themselves and attributions made to Puerto
Rican women in general. What are the two main factors leading to
this gap?

(pp. 248-249)   3.   What was the main focus of Rivera-Ramos' study on the perception of women's productivity in the workplace?

(pp. 250-251)   4.   In reference to the study on the perceptions of women's productivity in the workplace, the author mentions the general stereotype men hold about women. What is it?

(pp. 252)   5.   Compare and contrast some of the differences between unionized and non-unionized subjects in Rivera-Ramos' study on job-related stress.

(pp. 253-254)   6.   In the general conclusion, the author discusses various ways to deal with prejudice and discrimination in the work place. Briefly describe each recommendation.

(pp. 248)   7.   Explain the experience hypothesis discussed in the attitudes and perceptions.

(pp. 249-250)   8. Males and females differed on the amount of productivity they attributed to each gender.   What was the perception that was common to all respondents?

(pp. 252-253)   9. According to Rivera-Ramos, how did stressful working experiences show their consequences?

(pp. 253-254)   10. Is the social control exerted by stereotypes internal or external? Please explain.

Acculturation of Hispanics
George Domino

Multiple Choice

(pp. 256-257)

1. _____ refers to the myriad aspects and processes whereby an individual or group of individuals from one culture enters a different culture for an extended period of time.
   a. accommodation
   b. acculturation
   c. assimilation
   d. acclamation

(pp. 256-257)

2. _____ refers to an abandonment of traditional values, whereas _____ refers to a gradual process of coming to grips with a new culture one has entered.
   a. accommodation; acculturation
   b. adaptability; accommodation
   c. abandonment; adaptability
   d. assimilation; acculturation

(pp. 258-259)

3. "Racism will end only when capitalism is destroyed" is a statement with the _____ model of acculturation?
   a. Marxist
   b. Internal-Colony
   c. damaging culture
   d. assimilation

(pp. 257-258)

4. Historically, acculturation in the US has gone through three major phases. Which one of the following is *NOT* one of them?
   a. the "melting pot"
   b. Americanization
   c. political correctness
   d. cultural pluralism

(pp. 259-260)

5. Maria, a Hispanic immigrant, strictly retains her native culture. Anna, also a Hispanic immigrant, has let go of the beliefs and behaviors of her native culture. Which of the following acculturation models argues that Maria will experience more adjustment problems than Anna?
   a. adjustment and bicultural model
   b. acculturative stress model

c.   assimilationist model

d.   damaging culture model

(pp. 260-261)   6.   A characteristic of acculturation is the course it takes. Which of the following is **NOT** one of the phases to this process?

a.   integration

b.   adaptation

c.   contact

d.   conflict

(pp. 261-262)   7.   Angel, a Hispanic immigrant, is learning to speak English while Debbie, her Anglo co-worker is learning to speak Spanish. Debbie and Angel spend their lunch breaks together coaching each other in their newly acquired language. Debbie and Angel are reducing or eliminating conflict by becoming more like each other. This is an example of _____ .

a.   adjustment

b.   integration

c.   extinction

d.   ethnic loyalty

(pp. 261-262)   8.   _____ refers to knowing one's own culture and language, whereas _____ refers to the preference for one cultural orientation over the other.

a.   language preference; ethnocentrism

b.   cultural pluralism; cultural awareness

c.   cultural awareness; cultural loyalty

d.   ethnocentrism; egocentrism

(pp. 256-257)   9.   Acculturation may be viewed as a _____ phenomenon.

a.   group

b.   immediate

c.   individual

d.   both a and c

(pp. 262-263)   10.   One way to measure degree of acculturation is through generational distance. Generational distance is defined by _____.

a.   the distance in miles between the home of the respondent and that of the immigrants parents

b.   the age difference between the respondent and their children

c.   where the respondent and family members were born

d.   the birth order of the respondent

Short Answers

(pp. 256-257)   1. Compare and contrast integration and assimilation.

(pp. 256-258)   2. State three reasons why acculturation should be studied.

(pp. 258-259)   3. Briefly describe the way the internal-colony model sees Hispanics.

(pp. 260-261)   4. What are four characteristics of acculturation?

(pp. 261-262)   5. Compare and contrast cultural awareness with ethnic loyalty.

(pp. 262-263)   6. What is the assumption about third-generation Mexican Americans versus first generation Mexican Americans according to the definition of generational distance?

(pp. 262-263)   7. According to Ortiz and Arce, how will a lower status Mexican American who speaks Spanish predominantly be likely to differ from a higher status Mexican American who speaks Spanish predominately?

(pp. 263-264)   8. Name and give an example for each of the three types of items typically used in an acculturation scale.

(pp. 265-266)   9. What are two general criticisms of acculturation scales?

(pp. 266)   10. What is one reason why studying acculturation at work is important?

Native-American Psychology

❖   ❖   ❖

The American Indian Experience
Susan Shown Harjo

Multiple Choice

(pp. 275)   1. The experience of Native Americans is opposite from most other
minorities because:
   a. they have tirelessly demanded equal rights from the beginning of
their struggle with European invaders
   b. they have always been able to find their own niche in the great
"melting pot"
   c. they struggle to avoid being subjugated and attempt to preserve
their unique traditions
   d. they accept their struggle as being an inherent part of the natural
order of the universe

(pp. 275-276)   2. Which two treaties promised that no land would be taken without the
consent of the American Indians?
   a. Indian Removal Act and Ordinance for the Regulation of Indian
Affairs
   b. Indian Child Welfare Act and Northwest Ordinance
   c. Ordinance for the Regulation of Indian Affairs and the Northwest
Ordinance
   d. Non intercourse Acts and the Indian Land Consolidation Act

(pp. 275-276)   3. Why were lands east of the Mississippi stolen more frequently from
Native Americans during the first half of the 19th century?
   a. the west was not considered habitable by whites
   b. whites were intimidated by the violent war-like nature of Native
American tribes common in the west
   c. whites did not possess the means of transportation necessary to
reach the west
   d. very few American Indians lived west of the Mississippi

(pp. 276-277)   4.   After the US invaded a Sioux tribe stealing their land and resources, a concerted effort was made to transform the natives into "whites". According to the article, this is an example of:
a.   philanthropy
b.   cultural genocide
c.   acculturation
d.   integration

(pp. 277-278)   5.   Which is not a reason for the immense land loss by Native Americans since 1887?
a.   flooding for Corps of engineers projects
b.   taking of land for tax defaults and welfare payments
c.   invalidation of wills
d.   religious sites

(pp. 277-278)   6.   American Indians were encouraged by the mainstream culture to become farmers so as to:
a.   significantly contribute to the agricultural resources of the US
b.   supply the Native Americans with a livelihood which could provide them self worth
c.   cause them to become "more civilized"
d.   create a commonalty among land owners all over the US

(pp. 277-278)   7.   The phenomenon of Native Americans owning literally square inches land is a result of which plan implemented by the US government:
a.   1887 Allotment Act
b.   Indian Land Consolidation Act
c.   inheritance system
d.   "termination period"

(pp. 278-279)   8.   In 1956, Dorothy and her family were forced from their reservation in Utah to a high-rise housing project in Chicago. Based on this example, the era in which this scenario takes place is:
a.   post WW II
b.   termination period
c.   transference period
d.   assimilation era

(pp. 280)   9.   The criterion of "centrality" in regards to Native American religion is defined as:
a.   a place or monument which is actively worshipped at least once a week
b.   a naturally occurring monument such as a lake or tree

        c.   is not well defined, nor recognized by mainstream US culture
        d.   easily proven if the worship site may be photographed

(pp. 280-281)   10. According to the 1980 census, American Indians suffer from alcoholism at a rate _____ % higher than the rest of the population.
        a.   451
        b.   300
        c.   77
        d.   110

Short Answers

(pp. 275)   1. In your opinion, what factors have contributed to the fact that American Indians' experience is the reverse of other minorities in the United States?

(pp. 275-276)   2. What was the first Indian law passed by the first Congress of the US? What did it state?

(pp. 276-277)   3. How does the author feel about the process of assimilation, and its effect on Native Americans?

(pp. 276-277)   4. In what three ways did the US attempt to reach its goals of assimilation of the American Indians?

(pp. 276-277)   5. What fund was established in 1819 to provide education to Native Americans? What was the trade-off for Indians in return for obtaining this funding?

(pp. 276-277)   6. Why did the mainstream society set up boarding schools for American Indian children?

(pp. 277)   7. What is the Bureau of Indian Affairs (BIA)? What role has it played in Native American policy?

(pp. 275-281)   8. What do you remember learning about Native Americans in high school? How has your perspective changed?

(pp. 277-278)   9.   Describe the "inheritance system." How has this system adversely effected Native Americans?

(pp. 278-279)   10.   What is the "termination period?" How is this time in history characterized?

Pulling Coyote's Tale: Native American Sexuality and Aids
Terry Tafoya

Multiple Choice

(pp. 282-283)   1. Blood quantum is a way of tracking
- a. American Indians
- b. Alaskan Americans
- c. Latino Americans
- d. Both a and b

(pp. 281-282)   2. Native Americans became citizens of the United States in
- a. 1985
- b. 1988
- c. 1990
- d. 1924

(pp. 282-283)   3. The Indian Child Welfare act of 1977 was an attempt to:
- a. insure all Native American children an education
- b. halt the illegal use of Native American children in the laborers
- c. to stop the wholesale removal of Native American children from their families or tribes for the purpose of adoptions by Whites
- d. place more Native American children into non-Indian homes

(pp. 282-283)   4. Relocation is defined as:
- a. the removal of Native Americans off their reservations into major urban centers, cities
- b. moving from one reservation to another
- c. moving into rural areas
- d. relocating California Indians to Alaska

(pp. 285-287)   5. A "berdache" is:
- a. an individual with no specific gender
- b. considered inhuman
- c. a spirit
- d. an outcast

(pp. 284-285)   6. Females make up _____ percentage of the reported AIDS cases among Native Americans.
- a. 10%
- b. 50%

c   15%

d.   50%

(pp. 287-288)   7.   The term homosexual came into use in _____ as a _____ term.

a.   1860, identifying

b.   1869, medical

c.   1900, urban

d.   1965, slang

(pp. 285-287)   8.   According to Dr. Kathleen Toomey's unpublished study, _____ out of _____ gay American Indian men tested for the HIV antibody were IV drug users.

a.   30, 100

b.   30, 40

c.   30, 60

d.   60, 100

(pp. 282-283)   9.   The author say that it is misleading to conceptualize Native Americans as belonging to one culture, language or religion because:

a.   there are less than 2 different American Indian Tribes

b.   there are more than 250 different Indian languages?

c.   Native Americans were acculturated because of relocation

d.   all the above

(pp. 287-288)   10.   Traditionally, if an individual is responsible in meeting the obligations of the extended family network, their personal sexual behavior is:

a.   directed by the family

b.   controlled by the family

c.   controlled by the elders

d.   considered a personal choice by the tribe

Short Answers

(pp. 281)   1. What are some of the difficulties in providing adequate resources for AIDS preventative care to Native Americans?

(pp. 283-284)   2. Dr. Ben Muneta stated that the average life span of his Navajo patients with AIDS between diagnosis and death is six weeks. Discuss the reasons he give for such a short life span.

(pp. 281)   3. Give two reason why Native Americans are ethnic minorities.

(pp. 281-282)   4. What make American Indians and Alaskan Natives unique from other ethnic minorities?

(pp. 281)   5. What are the parallels between the Native Americans historical experience with Whites and their diseases and the gay and bisexual experience of AIDS. Discuss one.

(pp. 283-284)   6.   List two of the difficulties in tracking AIDS? cases in the Native American community.

(pp. 285-287)   7.   Briefly explain the Native American concept of gender and sexual behavior.

(pp. 284-285)   8.   Why is the data on reported AIDS cases for Native Americans misleading? Discuss briefly.

(pp. 287-288)   9.   Discuss briefly how the influence of Western homophobia may cause an individual to lead "double lives".

(pp. 285-288)   10.   Why are Native American street youth in urban areas a high risk population?

Native Americans: Adapting, yet Retaining
Martin Brokenleg and David Middleton

Multiple Choice

(pp. 289-290)   1. The illustrative episode at the beginning of this unit is followed by:
a. an analysis of the episode
b. three possible perceptions of the episode that differ in perspective
c. three possible perceptions of the episode held by the relatives of the deceased
d. a critique of the hospital staff's treatment of Tom Bear and his family

(pp. 290-291)   2. Native-American identity is better defined in terms of:
a. genetics
b. race
c. culture
d. federal and tribal law

(pp. 290-291)   3. Traditional Native American peoples:
a. all believe in an afterlife
b. all tell the story of *Wanagi Makoce*
c. vary in their beliefs, but see the body in the same way
d. have values and beliefs that vary from nation to nation

(pp. 291-292)   4. The author has chosen to focus on:
a. Native-American religious life
b. the amalgam of both Christian and tribal elements in the Sioux Nation
c. the tribal beliefs of the Lakota
d. the story of Tom Bear

(pp. 295-296)   5. The Lakota have a long history of the use of _____ in semireligious social settings.
a. marijuana
b. peyote
c. tobacco
d. alcohol

(pp. 292-293)   6. A paradigm is:
a. a religious symbol
b. a religious object

      c.   a Native-American concept

      d.   a model for processing information

(pp. 292-293)   7.   A central concept in the Lakota belief system and the way they cope with death is:

      a.   family cohesiveness

      b.   that the body of the deceased is an empty shell

      c.   punishment in the afterlife for sins committed during one's life

      d.   the consumption of alcohol

(pp. 293-295)   8.   The Lakota funeral may be described as:

      a.   a small, intimate gathering of the immediate family

      b.   an open ceremony with many people

      c.   primarily a ritual performed by the medicine man of the tribe

      d.   a ritual closed to outsiders

(pp. 296-297)   9.   The Lakota period of mourning lasts:

      a.   three days

      b.   at least one year

      c.   through the winter

      d.   none of the above

(pp. 297)   10.   The author concludes by suggesting, among other things, that:

      a.   the Lakota people have adapted to Christian and modern trends, yet retained their belief system

      b.   institutions should be equipped to accommodate the Lakota extended family

      c.   a failure to meet the familial needs of the Lakota results in institutionalized racism

      d.   all of the above

Short Answers

(pp. 289-290)   1.   Compare and contrast the three "possible perceptions" of the story of Tom Bear.

(pp. 290-291)   2.   How does the author suggest that Native-American identity be defined, and why?

(pp. 290-291)   3.   Describe the significance of the tribe to the Native-American identity.

(pp. 291-292)   4.   According to the Lakota religious belief system, who goes to the Spirit Land (afterlife) and how does one earn the right to go there?

(pp. 291-292)   5.   What is the Lakota perspective on the body? The soul?

(pp. 292)   6.   How are Lakota children educated about death and grief?

(pp. 292-295)   7.   Describe the significance of the family in the Lakota belief system, especially as it relates to mourning.

(pp. 293-297)   8. In the Lakota culture, what is done with the possessions of the deceased?

(pp. 296-297)   9. What is wanagi yuha?

(pp. 297)   10. In your opinion, what can contemporary institutions do to adapt to the Lakota way of mourning?

Native American Healing and Purification Rituals for War Stress

Steven M. Silver and John P. Wilson

Multiple Choice

(pp. 298)   1. Since the end of World War II, there has been a resurgence of Native-American culture with an emphasis on _____.
a. traditional healing and purification practices
b. the nature of war and its detrimental effects
c. sweat lodge rituals
d. the arts of pottery and jewelry making

(pp. 298-299)   2. Unlike many traumatic experiences, war has the potential for producing a form of emotional _____ in its participants.
a. depression
b. chaos
c. numbing
d. addiction

(pp. 298-299)   3. To regain both a sense of emotion and _____ is a central problem for any combatant.
a. self esteem
b. morality
c. remorse
d. serenity

(pp. 299-300)   4. "Sanctuary Trauma" is defined by Silver as:
a. trauma which is unusual and not confined to a particular place and time
b. the breaking down of the religious institutions of a culture
c. individual as a result of war
d. the incongruence between the actual sand idealized view of the post-trauma world.

(pp. 301-302)   5. A warrior whose tribe engaged in a full-fledged war only once in the history of their existence is the
a. Cheyenne
b. Apache
c. Papago
d. Iroquois

(pp. 302-303)   6.   A perspective shared by all tribes, regardless of their attitude about war is that:
  a.   every tribe member should participate in combat at least once in his/her lifetime
  b.   the warrior is recognized as sacrificing for the benefit of the tribe
  c.   the warrior should simply not bother returning to the tribe, for he will always carry the stigma of having disrupted the natural order
  d.   all warriors may return home, but only after they have cleansed themselves by wandering aimlessly for at least 15 days, speaking to no one

(pp. 302-303)   7.   An honored warrior who returned home from battle was isolated in his tent and forbidden to touch or feed himself. This practice is called:
  a.   cruel and unusual
  b.   a necessary method for reminding the warrior of his wrongdoing
  c.   a process by which "psychic numbing" is externalized and dealt with
  d.   a way for the warrior's family to observe firsthand some of the hardships he endured.

(pp. 305)   8.   A Viet Nam veteran who recently returned from the war was found huddled in the corner of his room making slow and methodical chicken scratches on his right arm with a safety pin. According to this article, the vet is probably experiencing:
  a.   a fear of losing his right arm
  b.   manic-depression
  c.   survivor guilt
  d.   PTSD

(pp. 305-306)   9.   The key difference which distinguishes the pow-wows of the Inter-Tribal Association from other pow-wows is that they
  a.   only occur at night
  b.   require a minimum of 25 people in order to be considered "official"
  c.   recognize, honor, and heal a specific group
  d.   serve as the focal point for social gathering

(pp. 307-308)   10.   Which of the following is **NOT** a psychological dimension afforded by the sweat lodge ceremony:
  a.   collective suffering and sharing
  b.   rebirth and renewal
  c.   focused attention on inner state
  d.   urge to remain in the womb-like atmosphere

Short Answers

(pp. 298-299)   1. What are some of the universal effects of war regardless of cultural background?

(pp. 299-300)   2. Why is it difficult for non-Indian mental health professionals to "hear" what Native American healers have to say?

(pp. 300-301)   3. What is the purpose of "War Dances"?

(pp. 301-302)   4. Compare and contrast the differing approaches to war held by the Iroquois, Apache, Cheyenne, and Papago tribes.

(pp. 302-303)   5. List the functions served by tribal ceremonies in preparing warriors for battle.

(pp. 303-304) 6. Define the term "mythos". Why is it important?

(pp. 304-305) 7. Describe the process of "reframing".

(pp. 305-306) 8. Discuss the functions served by the involvement of the families and community in healing ceremonies.

(pp. 305-306) 9. Discuss some differences in attitudes toward Viet nam vets by mainstream American and Native Americans.

(pp. 309-311) 10. Discuss briefly one or two psychological dimensions of how sweat lodge ceremonies have been beneficial to patients suffering from PTSD.

Counseling Intervention and American Tradition: An Integrative Approach

Theresa D. LaFramboise, Joseph E. Trimble and Gerald V. Mohatt

Multiple Choice

(pp. 315-316)   1.   For American Indians the term "Medicine" refers to:
    a.   a healing system integrating various aspects of well being
    b.   a variety of pharmaceuticals ranging from hacion to peyote
    c.   any substance which when invested alleviates pain or discomfort
    d.   a unique collection of herbs and otherwise nontraditional healing substances

(pp. 315-316)   2.   Among Native-Americans, it is _____ and _____ which are seen as most likely causing psychological or physical problems:
    a.   strong will; inability to adapt
    b.   low self–esteem; negative childhood experience
    c.   human weakness; lack of discipline in maintaining "community"
    d.   predisposition to depression; alcoholic tendencies

(pp. 317)   3.   The goal of therapy from a healing perspective is to:
    a.   strengthen the client's ego
    b.   encourage the client to transcend the ego
    c.   allow the client's inner motivations and unique experiences to be revealed
    d.   reach a clear, categorical diagnosis for the client's mental illness

(pp. 317-318)   4.   According to the author, a counselor who's aim is to help Native-Americans, but whose interest turns into an obsession, is demonstrating:
    a.   altruism
    b.   pathology
    c.   empathy
    d.   missionary zeal

(pp. 319-320)   5.   The neo-rogerian verbal response style, "facilitative communication", traditionally useful in establishing rapport between client and counselor was found by Atkinson, Morton & Sue ·1989) to be:
    a.   useful for native americans but not effective for ethnic minorities in general

    b.   useful for most ethnic minorities except native americans

    c.   ineffective for most ethnic minorities, including native americans

    d.   effective for most all american ethnic minorities

(pp. 321-322)   6.   The movement to revive Indian community empowerment (i.e. revitalizing Native-American culture, developing skills in order to develop an effective support system, etc.) has been labeled:

    a.   retraditionalization

    b.   acculturation

    c.   self–determination

    d.   empowerment movement

(pp. 322)   7.   According to Spindler & Spindler (1958), an "assimilated" american Indian:

    a.   speaks very little english and observes "old time" traditions and values

    b.   is unable to live either with their cultural group or the dominant society

    c.   cannot fully accept dominant traditions or values

    d.   has generally embraced dominant culture and values

(pp. 322-323)   8.   Which category of "indianness" is said to lead to greater cognitive functioning and self-actualization being:

    a.   bicultural

    b.   marginal

    c.   traditional

    d.   assimilated

(pp. 322-323)   9.   The central problem with person-centered therapy which makes it inappropriate for counseling Native-Americans is:

    a.   the focus on the client's family

    b.   the lack of consideration of the client's place within

    c.   the emphasis it places on the restraint of emotions

    d.   the low attrition rate of Indian clients

(pp. 324-325)   10.   The counselor assumes the role of a "catalyst" in which approach to:

    a.   social learning

    b.   network

    c.   behavioral

    d.   person-centered

Short Answers

(pp. 316-318)   1. What role do traditional ceremonies play in the lives of Native-Americans? In contrast, how are these rituals viewed by non-Indians?

(pp. 315-316)   2. What is the role of the family of a client in his/her healing process?

(pp. 317-318)   3. Describe the difference between a patronizing attitude and missionary zeal. What do they have in common?

(pp. 318-319)   4. Briefly discuss the two problems with conducting "value free" therapy with Native-American clients.

(pp. 321-322)   5. Define "empowerment". What is its purpose and goal?

(pp. 321-322)   6. How is "retraditionalization" a future-oriented movement?

(pp. 323-324)   7. What are the strengths of the social learning theoretical orientation to therapy?

(pp. 325-326)   8. What are the three basic strategies for effective transcultural therapy?

(pp. 327-330)   9. Briefly discuss the five important questions for training programs in counseling psychology suggested by the authors.

(pp. 322)   10. Discuss the concept of "an Assimilated American Indian.

Key

Karenga, **Black Psychology**:
1(d); 2(a); 3(c); 4(b); 5(a); 6(b); 7(b); 8(d); 9(a); 10(a).

Baldwin, Brown and Hopkins, **The Black Self-Hatred Paradigm Revisited**:
1(c); 2(d); 3(b); 4(d); 5(b); 6(d); 7(c); 8(d); 9(a); 10(b).

Monteiro and Fuqua, **African-American Gay Youth**:
1(d); 2(c); 3(a); 4(d); 5(b); 6(d); 7(a); 8(b); 9(a); 10(c).

Monteiro, **African-Americans and Reading**:
1(d); 2(a); 3(b); 4(d); 5(c); 6(a); 7(b); 8(b); 9(d); 10(d).

Nobles, **Africanity and the Black Family**:
1(b); 2(a); 3(a); 4(d); 5(c); 6(a); 7(d); 8(c); 9(b); 10(d).

Tong, **Asian-American Psychology**:
1(a); 2(c); 3(a); 4(c); 5(a); 6(a); 7(a); 8(d); 9(a); 10(a).

Nagata, **The Transgenerational Impact of the Japanese-American Communities**:
1(b); 2(c); 3(c); 4(c); 5(a); 6(c); 7(a); 8(c); 9(b); 10(a)

Ho, **An Analysis of Domestic Violence in Asian-American Communities**.
1(d); 2(d); 3(d); 4(a); 5(a); 6(a); 7(a); 8(a); 9(a); 10(c)

Chung, **Death and Dying**:
1(b); 2(b); 3(c); 4(b); 5(c); 6(d); 7(d); 8(b); 9(d); 10(d).

Tong, **Chinese-American Culture**:
1(b); 2(d); 3(c); 4(d); 5(d); 6(a); 7(a); 8(c); 9(d); 10(d).

Padilla, **Synposis of the History of Chicano Psychology**:
1(c); 2(b); 3(c); 4(a); 5(d); 6(b); 7(d); 8(a); 9(c); 10(d).

Padilla and Lindholm, **Child Bilingualism**:
1(b); 2(c); 3(d); 4(a); 5(d); 6(c); 7(b); 8(d); 9(b); 10(a).

Cervantes and Ramirez, **Spirituality and Family Dynamics in Psychotherapy with Latino Children**:
1(b); 2(d); 3(d); 4(b); 5(c); 6(d); 7(b); 8(b); 9(d); 10(d).

Rivera-Ramos, **The Psychological Experience of Puerto Rican Women at Work**:
1(a); 2(c); 3(b); 4(d); 5(c); 6(a); 7(d); 8(b); 9(a); 10(c).

Domino, **Acculturation of Hispanics**:
1(b); 2(d); 3(a); 4(c); 5(b); 6(a.); 7(a.); 8(c); 9(d); 10(c).

Harjo, **The American Indian Experience**:
1(c); 2(c); 3(a); 4(b); 5(d); 6(c); 7(c); 8(b); 9(c); 10(a).

Tafoya, **Pulling Coyote's Tale: Native American Sexuality and AIDS**:
1(d); 2(d); 3(c); 4(a); 5(a); 6(c); 7(b); 8(c); 9(a); 10(d).

Brokenleg and Middleton, **Native American: Adapting Yet Retaining**:
1(b); 2(c); 3(d); 4(c); 5(c); 6(d); 7(a); 8(b); 9(b); 10(d).

Silver and Wilson, **Native American Healing and Purification Rituals for War Stress**:
1(a); 2(d); 3(b); 4(d); 5(b); 6(b); 7(c); 8(c); 9(c); 10(d).

LaFromboise, Trimble and Mohatt, **Counseling Intervention and American Indian Tradition**:
1(a); 2(c); 3(b); 4(d); 5(c); 6(a); 7(d); 8(a); 9(b); 10(b).